THE ADVENTURES OF
HERCULES

retold by Martin Powell

illustrated by
José Alfonso Ocampo Ruiz

coloured by
Jorge Gonzalez

Raintree

www.raintreepublishers.co.uk
Visit our website to find out
more information about
Raintree books.

To order:
☎ Phone +44 (0) 1865 888066
🖨 Fax +44 (0) 1865 314091
💻 Visit www.raintreepublishers.co.uk

Raintree is an imprint of Capstone Global Library Limited, a company incorporated in England
and Wales having its registered office at 7 Pilgrim Street, London, EC4V 6LB – Registered
company number: 6695582

"Raintree" is a registered trademark of Pearson Education Limited, under licence to Capstone
Global Library Limited

Text © Stone Arch Books 2009
First published by Stone Arch Books in 2009
First published in hardback amd paperback in the United Kingdom by Capstone Global Library
in 2010
The moral rights of the proprietor have been asserted.

Edited in the UK by Harriet Milles
Originated by Capstone Global Library Ltd
Printed in China by Leo Paper Products Ltd

ISBN 978 1 406 21422 2 (hardback)
14 13 12 11 10
10 9 8 7 6 5 4 3 2 1

ISBN 978 1 406 21427 7 (paperback)
14 13 12 11 10
10 9 8 7 6 5 4 3 2 1

British Library Cataloguing in Publication Data
Powell, Martin -- The adventures of Hercules
A full catalogue record for this book is available from the British Library.

Every effort has been made to contact copyright holders of material reproduced in this book. Any
omissions will be rectified in subsequent printings if notice is given to the publisher.

Disclaimer
All the internet addresses (URLs) given in this book were valid at the time of going to press.
However, due to the dynamic nature of the internet, some addresses may have changed, or sites
may have changed or ceased to exist since publication. While the author and publiher regret any
inconvenience this may cause readers, no responsibility for any such changes can be accepted by
either the author or the publisher.

CONTENTS

INTRODUCING (Cast of Characters) 4

CHAPTER 1 SON OF ZEUS 6

CHAPTER 2 DEATH OF A FRIEND 18

CHAPTER 3 THE KING'S COMMAND 28

CHAPTER 4 A MIGHTY BURDEN 42

CHAPTER 5 LEGENDS NEVER DIE 52

How to pronounce Greek names 64

Glossary 65

Hera and Hercules 66

Discussion questions 68

Writing prompts 69

Books in this series 70

Find out more 72

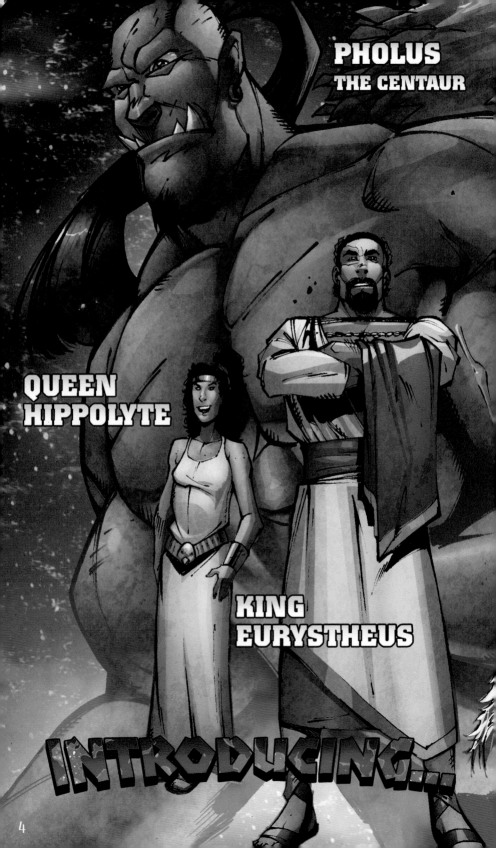

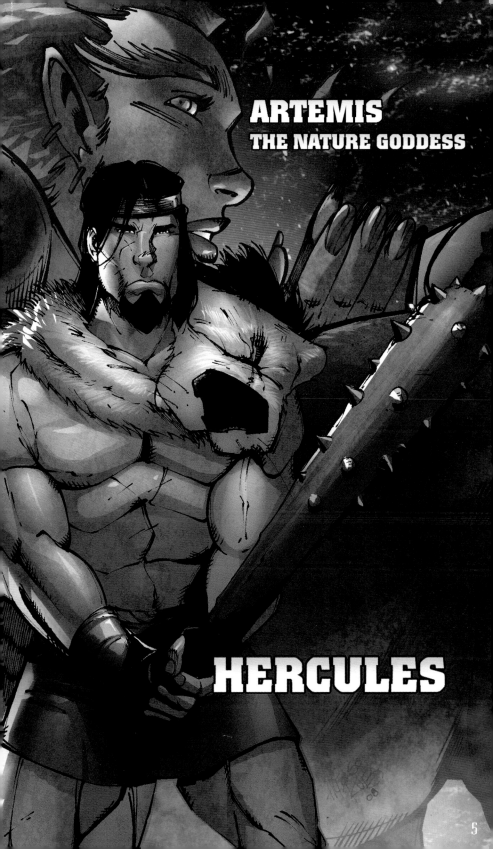

ARTEMIS
THE NATURE GODDESS

HERCULES

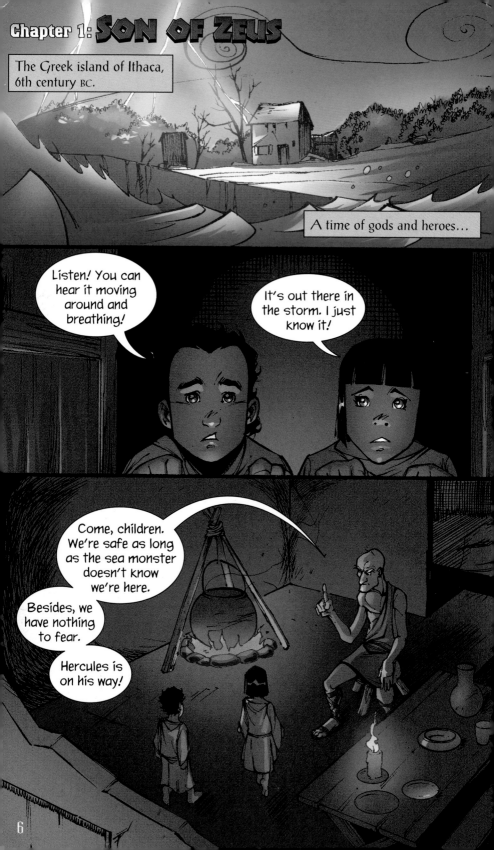

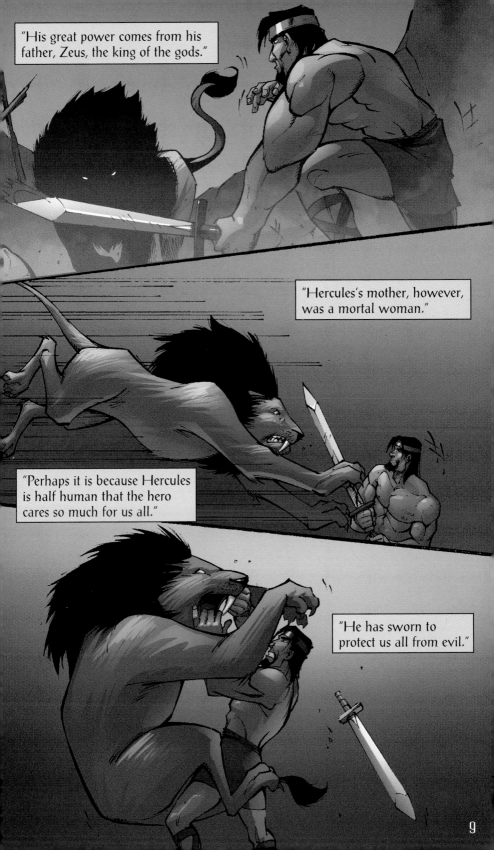

"His great power comes from his father, Zeus, the king of the gods."

"Hercules's mother, however, was a mortal woman."

"Perhaps it is because Hercules is half human that the hero cares so much for us all."

"He has sworn to protect us all from evil."

"Hercules fears nothing."

"Not even the invulnerable Nemean Lion, the killer of a thousand men!"

"Hercules quickly defeated the beast with his bare hands!"

It is accomplished. The first Labour.

"For his third Labour, Hercules had to hunt a magical deer that was sacred to the goddess Artemis."

"Finally, after tracking the mystical creature for over a year, Hercules caught sight of the sacred deer."

19

My pet will follow you, Hercules.

Complete your quest and return him to me unharmed.

Hercules brought the sacred deer to the king. Eurystheus became furious at the hero's triumph.

Why did Hercules serve that evil king, Grandfather?

Patience, child. All will be revealed.

But first, the fourth Labour of Hercules ...

... the hunt for the Giant Boar of Mount Erymanthus!

"Enraged by the death of his former teacher, Hercules flew into battle."

"His strength became unmatched."

"That day, the hero lost a great friend, but he won the respect of the centaurs."

Chapter 3: THE KING'S COMMAND

"Upon seeing evidence of Hercules's triumph, the king's jealousy grew."

"For the fifth Labour, the king was determined to humiliate the hero."

The king wants me to clean the stables in one day.

Why has the great Hercules been given the job of a cleaner?

The stables haven't been cleaned in over thirty years!

No point in putting it off any longer, then.

"And so, the task of cleaning the Augean Stables ..."

FWOOOOSHHH!!

" ... was solved by the clever mind and the mighty strength of Hercules ..."

SPLASH!

" ... in less than a single hour."

"Afterwards, Hercules travelled to Stymphalos."

"A flock of vampire birds had turned the village into a ghost town."

"First, Hercules had to find the birds."

"He used a pair of cymbals to bring them out of hiding."

"Then, his poisonous arrows silenced them forever."

"For his seventh Labour, Hercules had to capture the unstoppable Bull of Crete."

"By now, Hercules was used to doing the impossible."

"He stopped the Cretan Bull with a single blow."

BIIFF!

"As he carried the bull back to the king, the people celebrated his victorious return."

"The jealous king saw that his people had grown to love their new hero."

"Even the queen had begun to admire him."

"Eurystheus became desperate."

"He gave Hercules a Labour that would prove to be fatal for a mortal man."

"But mighty Hercules tamed the man-eating Mares of Diomedes with ease."

33

"The ninth Labour sent Hercules to an island populated by fearsome warriors."

"As Hercules landed alone upon the empty island, he felt eyes watching him."

"Suddenly ..."

Huh?!

THWIP!!

TINK!

WHAP!

POP!

34

"Hercules and Hippolyte became inseparable."

So, what's it like having the king of the gods as your father?

Zeus has not spoken to me since my mother died.

I am alone in the world.

No one should be alone.

Come walk with me.

Hercules, I know you seek my Magic Belt. I will gladly give it to you.

But I want to know why King Eurystheus controls you.

I serve him by command of Hera, the queen of the gods ...

... so that I may pay for my crimes.

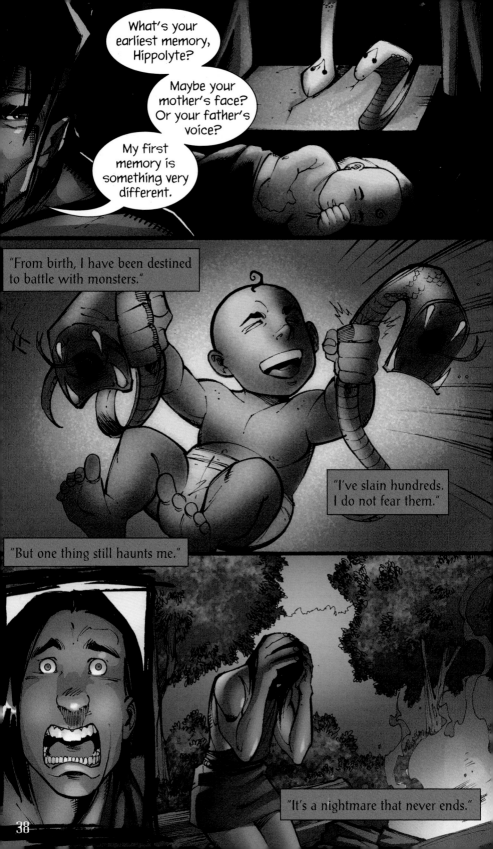

"Although I don't remember doing it, I once did something terrible."

"Hera told me I had destroyed my home village of Thebes during a nightmare."

"There were no survivors."

Hercules, Son of Zeus, behold what you have done!

"Hera ordered me to perform King Eurystheus's Twelve Labours."

"Only then will the gods forgive me."

"Hercules tried to do as Hippolyte had requested ..."

"But he wondered if he would ever be strong enough to forgive himself."

The Amazons still hunt him to this very day.

That's so sad, Grandfather.

Hercules didn't do anything wrong.

Indeed. And Hercules would have little time to grieve ...

... for his next Labour awaited him upon his return.

43

"Geryon, the evil grandson of Medusa, had stolen a herd of cattle from a nearby farm."

FWOOSH!

"Reasoning with the monster was simply not an option."

CRACK!!

"The mighty hero was forced to use his fists ... and his club."

"On his way to perform his eleventh Labour, Hercules finally met his match."

"Antaeus, son of Gaia."

None shall pass Antaeus the Earth Giant.

This mountain is forbidden, mortal. Leave now, or you will surely perish.

We'll see about that!

THUNK

"But the giant only rose again, and laughed."

Puny human.

"He had found Atlas the Titan!"

Son of Zeus, I know what you seek — the sacred Golden Apples!

Zeus has punished me for revolting against him. I have held the heavy sky upon my weary shoulders for ages.

I have no reason to help his son, the hero.

I refuse to tell you where the Golden Apples are.

You do not understand, noble Atlas. I come not to ask a favour, but to make a deal.

"He asked Atlas to hold up the sky for a moment so he could stretch his aching shoulders."

"Atlas laughed and agreed. "

Wait, Atlas!

"Hercules admitted defeat, but he had a final request."

"Hercules gathered up the Golden Apples ..."

"... and left Atlas to hold up the sky for the rest of eternity."

And that is how Hercules outwitted the Titan.

Hercules is as smart as he is strong!

That's true, and he would need his strength and brains for his final Labour.

"The twelfth Labour took Hercules deep into the Land of the Dead."

"The hero bravely ventured into the haunted cave."

"Hercules paid Charon, guide of the Lost Souls, to ferry him across the River Styx."

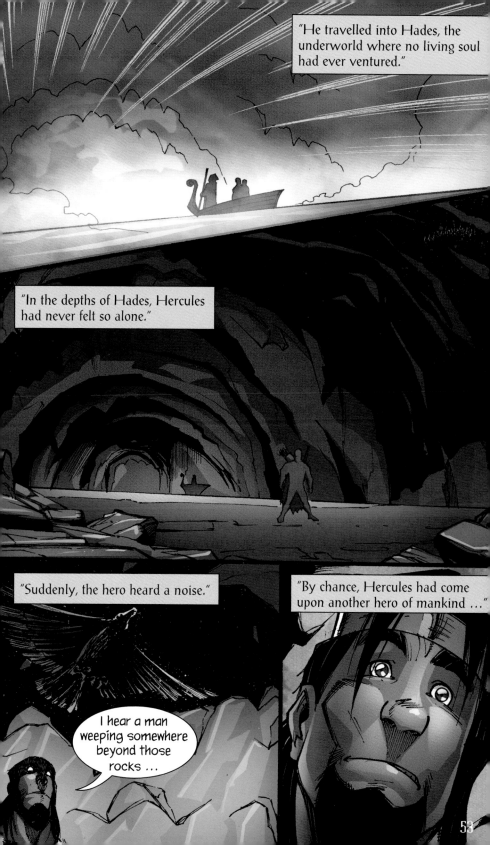

"He travelled into Hades, the underworld where no living soul had ever ventured."

"In the depths of Hades, Hercules had never felt so alone."

"Suddenly, the hero heard a noise."

"By chance, Hercules had come upon another hero of mankind ..."

I hear a man weeping somewhere beyond those rocks ...

53

"Hercules overpowered Cerberus ..."

"... and carried him back to the world of the living!"

"King Eurysthenes was terrified by Cerberus."

A ruler must be brave, Eurystheus. You're not worthy of your kingdom.

The people deserve someone braver — and wiser.

Take it away, I beg of you!

"The queen accepted the Magic Belt, and ruled her people wisely for the rest of her long life."

"Hercules returned Cerberus to Hades, and searched the lands for people in need of his help."

Of all the heroes who have walked on Earth ...

... none were as great as Hercules!

How to Pronounce Greek Names

Name	Pronunciation	Name	Pronunciation
Alcmene	alk-MEAN-eh	Hercules	HERK-yoo-leeze
Antaeus	an-TEE-uss	Hippolyte	hip-POL-eet-a
Artemis	AR-te-mis	Hydra	HIGH-dra
Athena	ah-THEE-na	Iphitus	IF-it-uss
Augean	aw-GAY-an	Ithaca	ITH-a-ca
centaur	SEN-tor	Lydia	LID-ee-a
Cerberus	SIR-ber-uss	Medusa	meh-DEW-sa
Charon	CARE-on	Mycenae	my-SEE-nee
Crete	KREET	Nemea	ne-MAY-a
Deianira	day-a-NEAR-ra	Omphale	om-FA-leh
Diomedes	die-o-MEE-deeze	Pholus	FO-luss
Erymanthus	air-ee-MAN-thuss	Prometheus	pro-MEETH-ee-uss
Eurystheus	yoo-RIS-the-uss	Stymphalos	stim-FA-loss
Gaia	GUY-ah	Styx	STICKS
Geryon	ga–RYE-on	Thebes	THEEBS
Hades	HAY-deeze	Titan	TIE-tan
Hera	HAIR-a	Zeus	ZOOCE

GLOSSARY

burden   heavy load that someone has to carry

centaur   creature that is half man, half horse

cymbals   musical instrument made of two circles of brass that makes a ringing sound

grieve   feel very sad because someone has died

eternity   for ever

heavenly bodies   the sun, moon, stars, and other objects in the sky

humiliate   make someone feel foolish or embarrassed

invulnerable   unable to be hurt or harmed

Labour   one of the tasks given to Hercules by King Eurysthenes. The king thought the Labours were impossible to carry out and he hoped they would destroy Hercules.

mortal   human, unable to live for ever

quest   mission

reputation   opinion people have of something or someone

sacred   holy

sear   burn

stables   building where animals such as horses or cattle are kept

Titan   one of a group of gods in Greek myths who ruled before Zeus came into power

trespass   enter or go somewhere without permission

underworld   place where people go when they die

vampire   creature that sucks people's blood

witness   someone who does not take part in an event but sees it and can tell others about it

HERA AND HERCULES

In Greek and Roman times, Hercules was one of the most celebrated mythical figures. Half human and half god, Hercules was the son of Zeus, the king of the gods, and Alcmene, a mortal woman. The goddess Hera, Zeus's wife, was angry that Zeus had fathered children with another woman. Since Hera could not harm Zeus, the king of the gods, she punished his son Hercules instead.

When Zeus learned that Alcmene was pregnant with Hercules, he announced that the next child born would be the new king. To ruin Zeus's plan, Hera caused a boy named Eurystheus to be born early, making him king instead of Hercules. This angered Zeus, but he stuck to his word and made Eurystheus king. Hera had robbed Hercules of his throne — and her revenge had only just begun.

Next, Hera made Hercules go temporarily insane. In this state, he did some horrible things. When he came to his senses, he visited the Oracle to find out how to redeem himself. Unfortunately, the Oracle was also being manipulated by Hera. The Oracle told him to serve King Eurystheus, who had him perform twelve difficult labours — all because of Hera's jealousy.

Years later, Hera once again sent a madness down upon Hercules. In his altered state of mind, he threw his best friend Iphitus over a wall, killing him. When Hercules realized what had happened, he pledged himself to Queen Omphale of Lydia. Again he hoped to atone for his tragic mistake, not knowing he was innocent.

After serving Omphale for a year, Hercules was free to do as he pleased. He went to the town of Thebes and married a woman named Deianira, and the two of them raised a family together. One day, a centaur named Nessus kidnapped Deianira. Hercules managed to shoot Nessus with an arrow tipped with poison from the blood of the Hydra. Near death, Nessus told Deianira to rub his blood on Hercules, which would make him love her forever. But Nessus had lied to her — his blood was poisoned from the arrow Hercules had shot him with, and the poisoned blood burned Hercules's flesh until he was near death.

As he died, Hercules was allowed into Olympus, the home of the gods, as a reward for his good deeds and as consolation for being the victim of Hera's trickery.

DISCUSSION QUESTIONS

1. Atlas refused to help Hercules because he didn't like Hercules's father. Is it fair to judge someone based on their family and friends?

2. At first, Hercules thinks a nightmare was to blame for his home town's destruction. Do you think dreams can cause people to do strange things? Is it possible to interpret dreams to find out what they mean? Why or why not?

3. Hercules faces off against many foes in his adventures. Which of his opponents was the most dangerous? Which enemy was the coolest? Why?

WRITING PROMPTS

1. Hera punished Hercules for something he didn't actually do. Have you ever been punished for something that you didn't do? How did it feel? Write about it.

2. Imagine that you are a super-powerful hero like Hercules. What will you do with your incredible strength? Will you compete in athletics? Help others? Write a story about your adventures.

3. Hercules was ordered to perform twelve impossible Labours. What if he had to do a thirteenth task? What would it be? What kind of challenge, or monster, would he face? Describe what happens.

BOOKS IN THIS SERIES

Jason and the Golden Fleece

Brave Jason comes to claim his throne, but the old king will not give up his rule so easily. To prove his worth, Jason must find the greatest treasure in the world, the Golden Fleece.

Perseus and Medusa

Young Perseus grows up, unaware of his royal birth. Before he can claim his heritage, the hero is ordered to slay a hideous monster named Medusa, whose gaze turns men into solid stone. How can the youth fight an enemy he cannot even look at?

Theseus and the Minotaur

The evil king of Crete demands that fourteen young Athenians be fed to the Minotaur, a creature that is half-man, half-bull. Only Prince Theseus can save them from the fearsome monster that lives deep in the maze-like Labyrinth.

The Adventures of Hercules

The son of a mortal woman and the king of the gods, Hercules is blessed with extraordinary strength. The goddess Hera commands that the mighty Hercules must undergo twelve incredible tasks to pay for a mistake he made in the past.

FIND OUT MORE

Websites

http://www.ancientgreece.co.uk/
Visit this British Museum site to find out more about ancient Greek civilization.

http://www.bbc.co.uk/schools/primaryhistory/ancient_greeks/
This site will help you to discover still more about how the ancient Greeks lived and worked. Click on the "Gods and Heroes" link for more fun facts about Greek heroes.

http://greece.mrdonn.org/greekgods/index.html
Find out about the roles and relationships of the ancient Greek gods. The Roman names for some of them are also given on this web page.

Books

Ancient Greece (New Explore History series), Jane Shuter (Heinemann Library, 2007)

Ancient Greece (Time Travel Guides series), Anna Claybourne (Raintree, 2008)

The Ancient Greeks (Understanding People in the Past series), Rosemary Rees (Heinemann Library, 2007)

The History and Activities of Ancient Greece (Hands-on Ancient History series), Greg Owens (Heinemann Library, 2007)

Welcome to the Ancient Olympics!, Jane Bingham (Raintree, 2008)